MW00714624

ABC
Order

By Lillian Lieberman
Illustrated by Corbin Hillam

Publisher: Roberta Suid
Editor: Elizabeth Russell
Cover Design: David Hale
Design and Production: Mary Francis

Entire contents copyright © 1984 by Monday Morning
Books, Box 1680, Palo Alto, California 94302

Permission is hereby granted to reproduce
student materials in this book for non-commercial
individual or classroom use.

ISBN 0-912107-12-X

Printed in the United States of America

9 8 7 6 5 4 3 2

INTRODUCTION

ABC ORDER presents worksheets, games, and bulletin boards to reinforce the learning of alphabetical order for primary children. Reproducible worksheets ask students to sequence letters of the alphabet while coloring, cutting, pasting, tracing, numbering, writing, and playing simple games.

Each activity sheet is coded to the specific sequencing order at the top of the page for easy teacher reference. Worksheets vary in difficulty, and more than one worksheet is provided for each skill for those who need more practice.

Students sequence both upper and lower case manuscript letters in *ABC ORDER*. Activities involve sequencing single letters and groups of letters, letters that precede, go between, and follow, and words according to first and second letters.

In addition to worksheets, *ABC ORDER* includes directions for bulletin boards and games. Teachers can create hands-on bulletin boards in which the whole class can be actively involved. Several card games offer further reinforcement in alphabetical sequencing. Letter cards are provided for the bulletin boards, card games, and individual practice.

Through gradual skill development and a variety of activities, *ABC ORDER* introduces and reinforces alphabetical order in preparation for later work in dictionary, vocabulary, spelling, and reference skills. The activities in *ABC ORDER* are designed to make the process of acquiring these skills fun.

Directions for Worksheets

1. Read aloud the directions for each worksheet. You may wish to ask a student to read to the class.
2. Demonstrate the specific directions for each page, such as cut, paste, color, trace, number, or write.

3. After children have completed directions, have them color each page.

Enrichment Activities

1. **Show What's Missing** Give each child a set of alphabet letter cards to arrange in order on his or her desk. On the chalkboard write a sequence of letters, with one or more missing before, between, or after other letters. Point to the missing letter or letters and say, "Show me." Students hold up the missing letter or letters in order. Write the correct letters on the chalkboard so that students can check themselves.

2. **ABC Bounce or Pass** To reinforce alphabetical order, have individual children say the alphabet in order as they bounce a ball in rhythm. For larger group involvement, have the class pass the ball around a circle as they say the alphabet in order. If someone drops the ball or misses a letter, the class must begin from A again.

3. **ABC Mix-up, Fix-up** Give four children alphabet letters in sequence. Have them stand facing the class with cards showing. Choose a fifth child to leave the room. While he or she is out, rearrange the first four so that their letters are in mixed order. Then the other child must rearrange the children and their letters in correct ABC order. If correct, the child gets to pick the next person to leave the room. Select four more children and letters for another round.

4. **Doggy Bones** Cut out dog bone shapes from oak tag or construction paper. With them make sets of words to alphabetize, each consisting of 3 or 4 words beginning with the same letter. Pick a student to be the "dog," another to be the "dog-catcher." Place a set of bones (words) on the chalk tray in random order. The dog-catcher must alphabetize the words, using the second letters. When the dog sees that the order is

correct, he or she runs to a safe spot indicated by the teacher. The dogcatcher tries to tag the dog before he or she reaches the safe spot. If tagged, the dog goes to the pound (the class group). If not tagged, the dog becomes the next dogcatcher. If the words are incorrectly arranged, the dog may rearrange them correctly and become the next dogcatcher. Good for a rainy day game.

Get on the ABC Train!

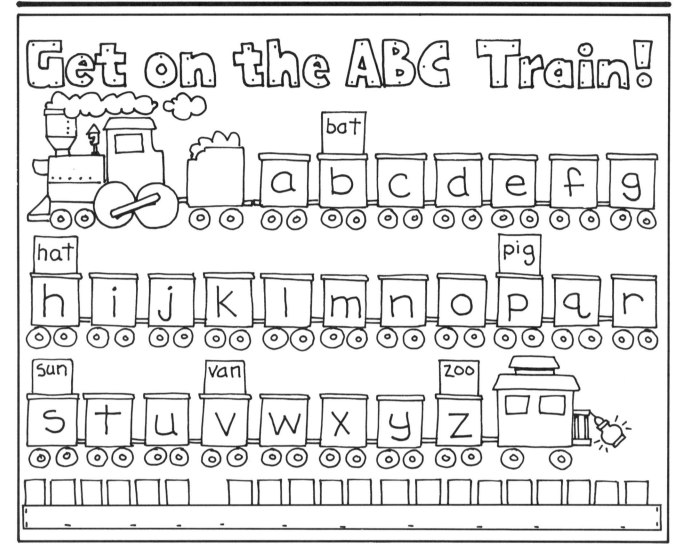

Objective:
To reinforce alphabetical sequencing skills

Materials:
Oak tag, yarn, bulletin board letters

Construction:
1. Duplicate train and alphabet letter cars. Mount them on oak tag for firmer backing.
2. Have students cut out and color their cars. Color the locomotive.
3. Draw lines and circles with black felt pen on long strip of oak tag for tracks, wheels.
4. Staple locomotive to bulletin board. Staple sides and bottom of long oak tag strip to form a holder. Add a similar oak tag holder at bottom of bulletin board.

5. Pin on title letters and circle with yarn.

Procedure:
1. Students place their alphabet letter cars in order on the train track. Entire class or individual student can name letter as it is placed. Repeat as many times as desired.
2. As alphabetical sequencing skills progress, take a few letters from the train and place in card holder at bottom. Students then take turns replacing cards correctly as they name the letters.
3. When students know alphabetical order, place word cards in holder to be sequenced. Pin letter cards on the track as a guide.

ABC Race To Win

ABC Race To Win!

won

wag   wig

fun

flag

cat   crib   cup

Objective:
To practice alphabetizing by second letter

Materials:
Colored construction paper, oak tag, black yarn, straight pins, bulletin board letters

Construction:
1. Cut three rectangular pockets from oak tag. Arrange in a vertical row on left side of bulletin board. Staple sides and bottoms to form holders for cars.
2. Cut three or more sets of three cards from construction paper. Write words that begin with the same letter on each set. Place cars in pocket holders.

3. Pin yarn to bulletin board to form race track. Add arrows and flags cut from construction paper. Pin on bulletin board letters to form title.

Procedure:
1. Students place three cars in each lane of the race track in correct alphabetical order, using the second letter of each word to determine sequence.
2. Change race car words as often as desired.
3. When students become more skilled, challenge them to alphabetize words by third letter.

Two In A Row

Objective:
To reinforce alphabetical sequencing skills

Materials:
1 set Alphabet Letter Cards

Procedure:
1. Three may play this game.
2. Dealer shuffles cards, deals five to each player, and places the rest face down in a "fish" pile.
3. Players look at their cards and pair up any two which come together in the alphabet. Pairs are called books and are placed face up in front of players.
4. First player asks player to left for a letter needed to make a book. If second player has it, first player takes it, reads letter sequence aloud, and makes a book. If letter sequence is incorrect, another player may challenge it and add those two cards to his or her hand.
5. If player to left does not have desired card, asking player takes a card from the "fish" pile and tries to make a book.
6. Game continues until all cards are played. First player to use all cards in hand is the first winner. Player who makes the most books is second winner.

Variation:
• Follow general directions to make three letter sequences.

Three In A Row

Objective:
To reinforce alphabetical sequencing skills

Materials:
1 set Alphabet Letter Cards

Procedure:
1. Three may play this game.
2. Dealer shuffles cards, deals eight to each player, and places last two cards face up in playing area.
3. Players look at their cards. Each player in turn places a card face up on the playing area. If the card forms a two letter sequence with any other card on the playing area, player must put it in order beside that card.
4. Players continue to put down cards, trying to complete three-letter sequences. Player who completes a three-letter sequence must name it in order to keep it as a book. Other players may challenge if they think sequence incorrect. Correct challenger gets to add cards to his or her hand.
5. Game continues until all cards are played. First winner uses up hand first. Second winner has the most letter sequence books.

Variation:
● Follow general directions, making four-letter sequences.

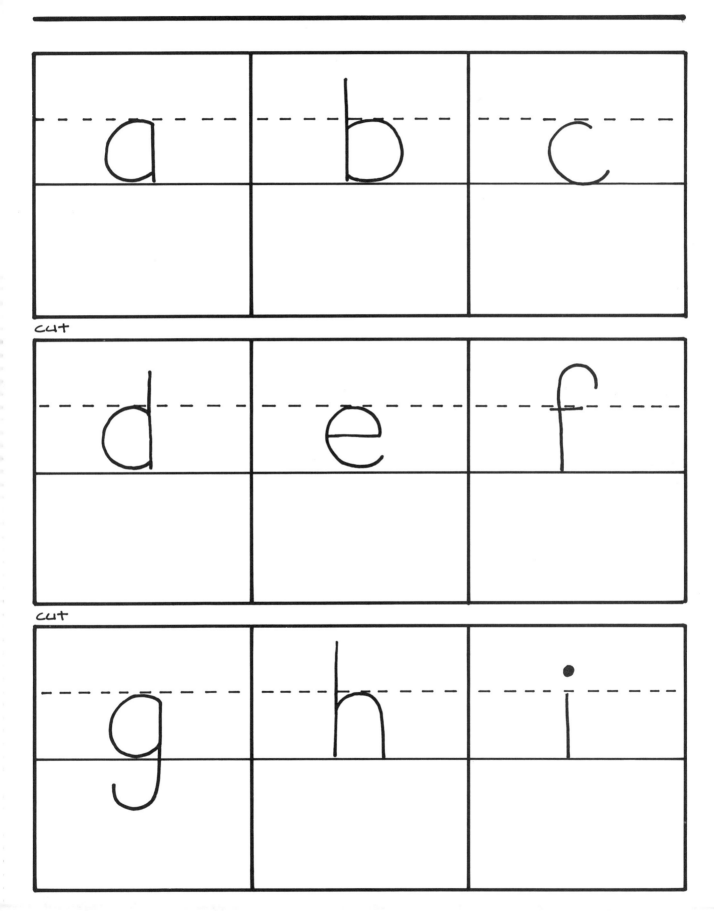

cut

cut

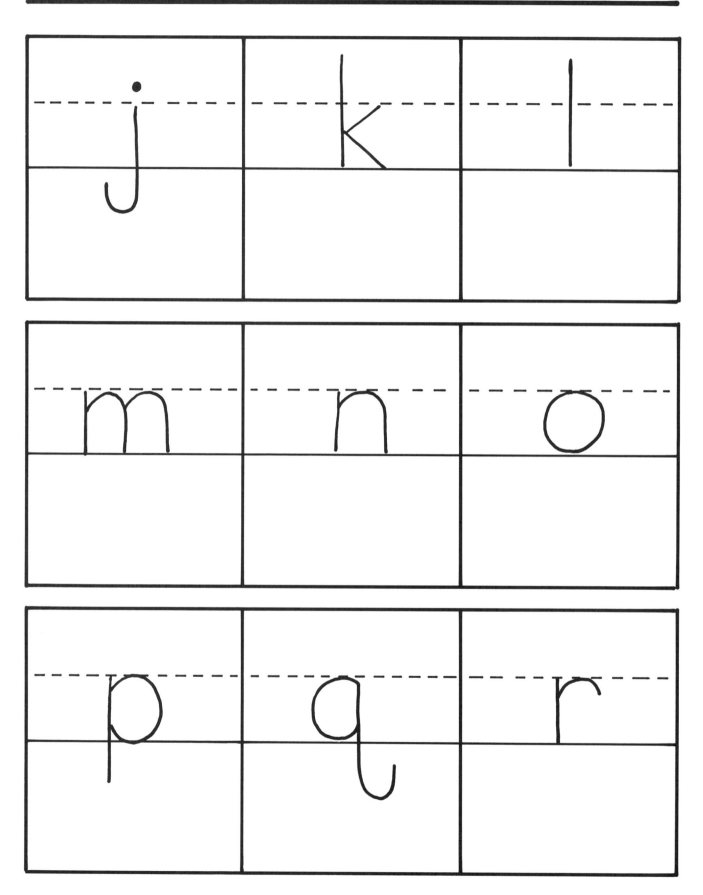

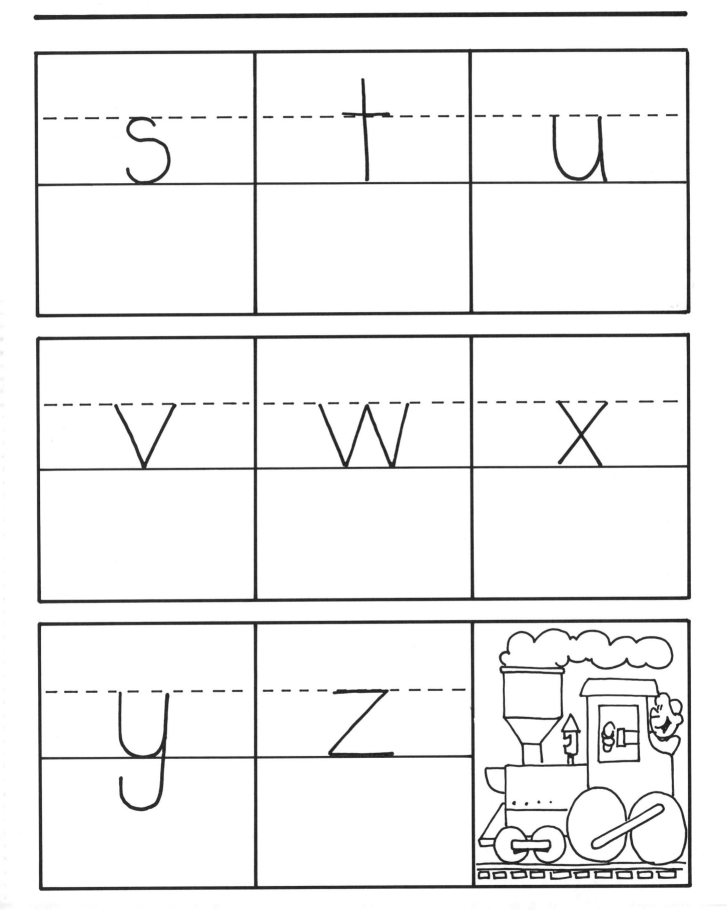

Name and trace the letters on the shooting stars.

F G S X

E Y Q W

A B P V N

C I O U Y

R H Z T

A G M S

ABC Order © 1984 Monday Morning Books

Skill: A – Z

Connect the kangaroo's rocks in abc order. Color.

ABC Order © 1984 Monday Morning Books

Skill: A - Z

Cut and paste the clotheslines in abc order. Color.

L M
J K
G H I

A B C D E F

N O P Q R S T

U V W X Y Z

14

ABC Order © 1984 Monday Morning Books

Help the computer! Fill in the missing letters. Color.

The screen shows:
A _ C _ E _ G _ I _
K _ M _ O _ Q _
S _ U _ W _ Y _

ABC Order © 1984 Monday Morning Books

Skill: A - Z

Name

Cut and paste the missing bottles in abc order. Color.

ABC Order © 1984 Monday Morning Books

Skill: ☐ B C

Cut and paste the missing cones in abc order. Color.

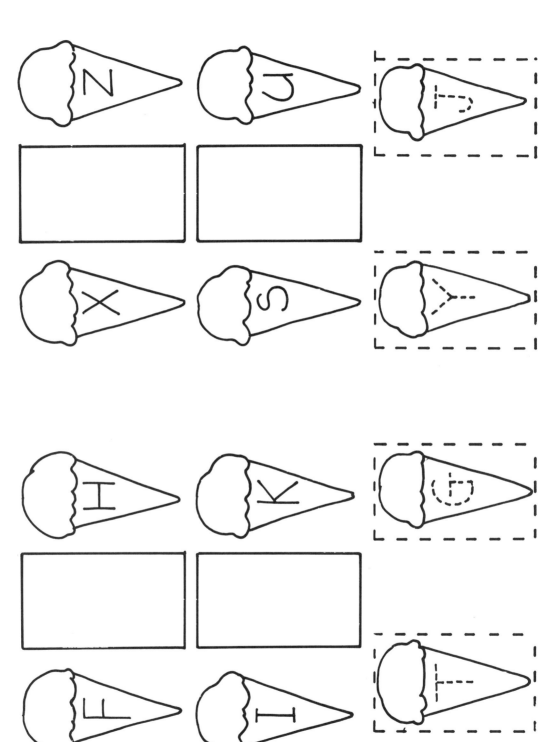

ABC Order © 1984 Monday Morning Books

Skill: A ☐ C

Cut and paste the letter that comes last. Color.

M N

I J

A B

Q R

ABC Order © 1984 Monday Morning Books

Skill: A B ☐

Write the first and last letters in abc order. Color.

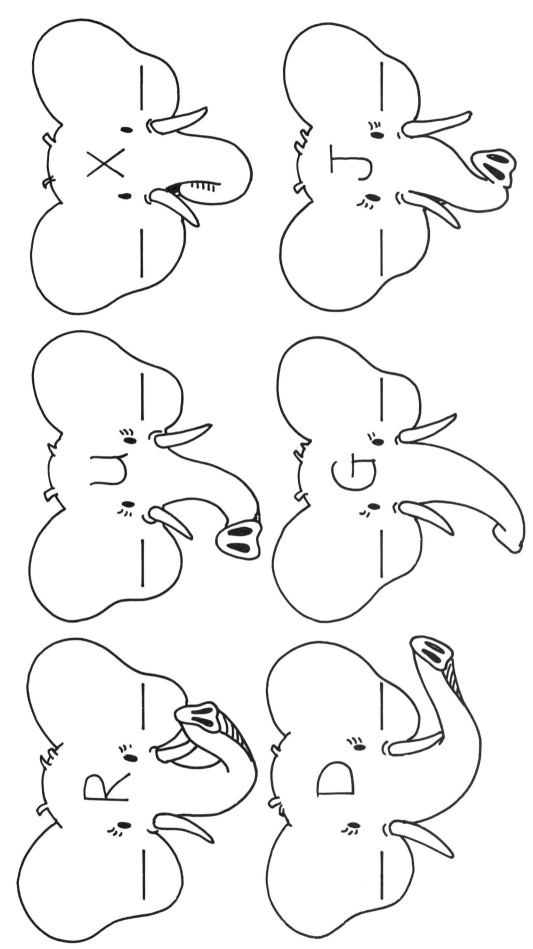

ABC Order © 1984 Monday Morning Books

Skill: ☐ B ☐

Name _____

Fill in the letters each caterpillar is missing. Color.

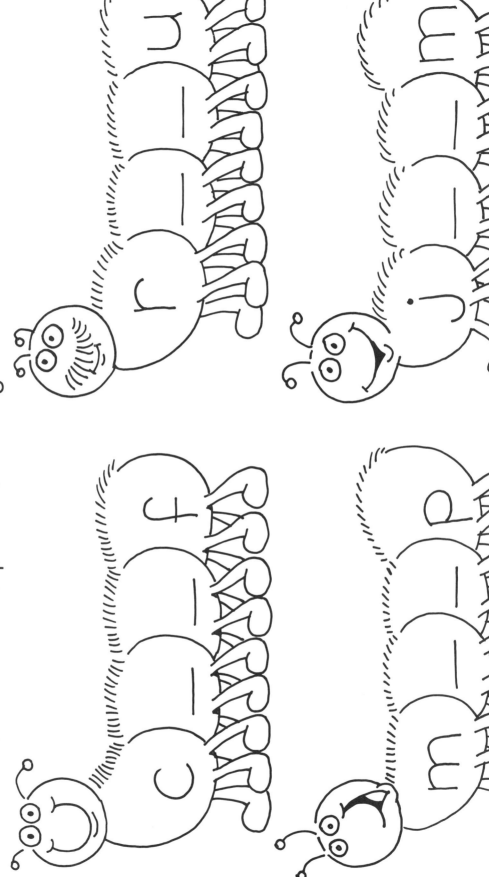

20

ABC Order © 1984 Monday Morning Books

Skill: A ☐ ☐ D

Name and trace the letters in the candy jar. Color.

ABC Order © 1984 Monday Morning Books

Skill: a - z

Cut and paste the missing letters in abc order. Color.

a	b	c	d	
		i	j	k
		l		
	q	r	s	t
			y	z

m n o p

e f g h

u v w x

Skill: a - z

ABC Order © 1984 Monday Morning Books

Cut and paste the letter that comes first in abc order.

c p

l m

j n z

ABC Order © 1984 Monday Morning Books

Skill: □ b c

Name _____

Cut and paste the cars that come first in abc order.

ABC Order © 1984 Monday Morning Books

Skill: ☐ b c

Name _____

Cut and paste the first letters in abc order. Color.

ABC Order © 1984 Monday Morning Books

Skill: □ b c

Write the missing first letters on the sundaes. Color.

ABC Order © 1984 Monday Morning Books

Skill: ☐ b c

Write the missing first letters on the balls. Color.

ABC Order © 1984 Monday Morning Books

Skill: □ b c

Name _____

Cut and paste the missing middle letters. Color.

c

m

e

p

e

o

g

r

c

a

d

f

ABC Order © 1984 Monday Morning Books

Skill: a ☐ c

Name _____

Cut and paste the missing middle letters. Color.

ABC Order © 1984 Monday Morning Books

Skill: a ▢ c

Cut and paste the missing middle letters in abc order.

X
□
V

W
□
Z

S
□
u

U

W

ABC Order © 1984 Monday Morning Books

Skill: a □ c

Name

Cut and paste the missing middle letters. Color.

 s

 c

l

u

u

e

o

t

n

q

h

p

 p

 g

 o

d

t

m

31

ABC Order © 1984 Monday Morning Books

Skill: a ☐ c

Write the missing middle letters in abc order. Color.

h — j

l — n

m — o

t — u — v

b — d

a — c — s

32

Write the missing middle letters in abc order. Color.

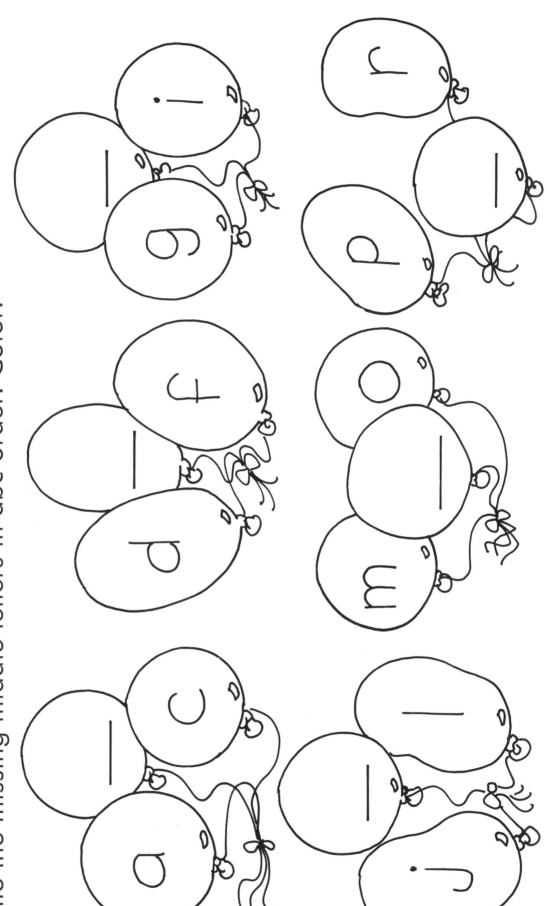

33

ABC Order © 1984 Monday Morning Books

Skill: a ☐ c

Cut and paste the missing last letters. Color.

b

c

e

k

f

ABC Order © 1984 Monday Morning Books

Skill: a b □

Cut and paste the missing last letters. Color.

35

ABC Order © 1984 Monday Morning Books

Name _____

Write the last letters on the fish in abc order. Color.

r_l s_t

b_l a

q_l e p

w_l v

j_l i

ABC Order © 1984 Monday Morning Books

Skill: a b ☐

Name _____

Cut and paste the missing first and last letters.

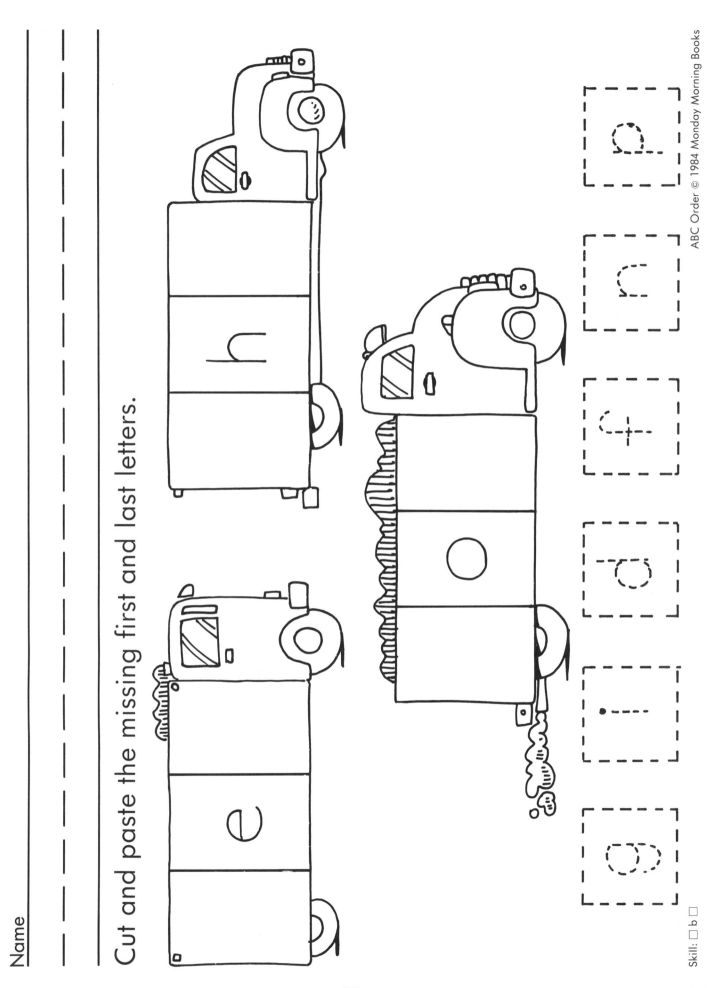

ABC Order © 1984 Monday Morning Books

Skill: ☐ b ☐

Cut and paste the missing first and last letters.

38

ABC Order © 1984 Monday Morning Books

Write the first and last letters in abc order. Color.

ABC Order © 1984 Monday Morning Books

Name _____

Cut and paste the missing middle letters in abc order.

ABC Order © 1984 Monday Morning Books

Skill: a ☐ ☐ d

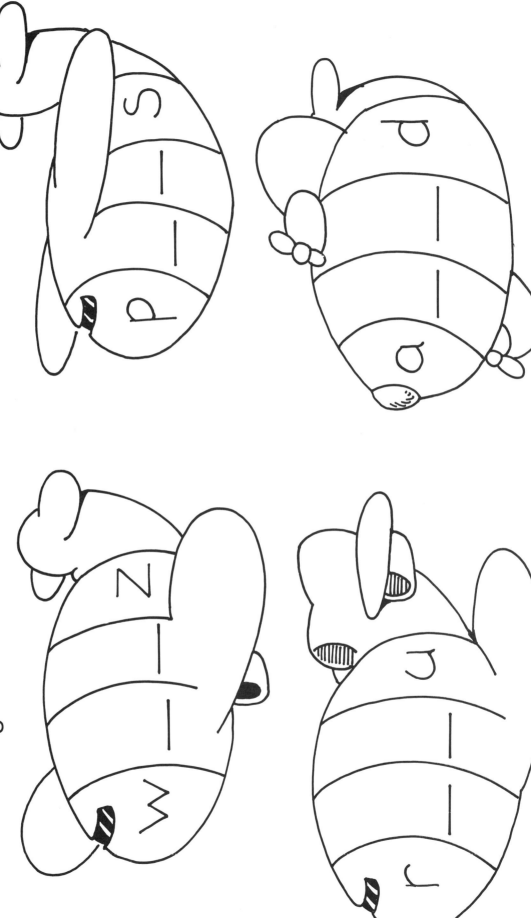

Name

Write the missing middle letters in abc order.

ABC Order © 1984 Monday Morning Books

Skill: a ☐ ☐ d

Cut and paste the missing first letters. Color.

o p

l m

y z

ABC Order © 1984 Monday Morning Books

Write the missing first letters in abc order. Color.

r

q ___

___

w x

___ z

m n

___ ___

43

ABC Order © 1984 Monday Morning Books

Cut and paste the missing last letters. Color.

44

ABC Order © 1984 Monday Morning Books

Cut and paste the missing last letters. Color.

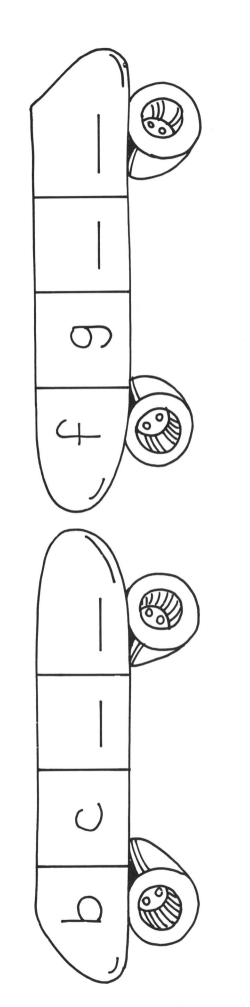

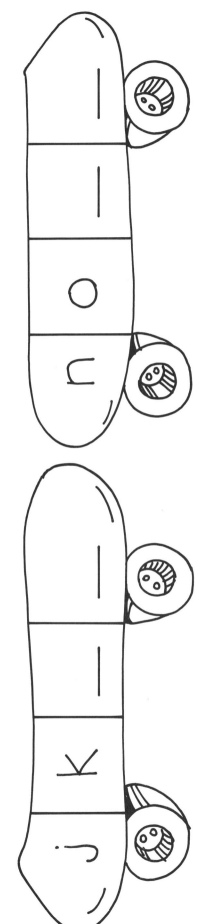

ABC Order © 1984 Monday Morning Books

Write the first and last letters in abc order. Color.

b c

m n

v w

r s

ABC Order © 1984 Monday Morning Books

Skill: ☐ b c ☐

Write the missing letters in abc order. Color.

t

___ ___ p

e
___ ___

ABC Order © 1984 Monday Morning Books

Skill: ☐ ☐ ☐ d

Write the missing letters on the balloons. Color.

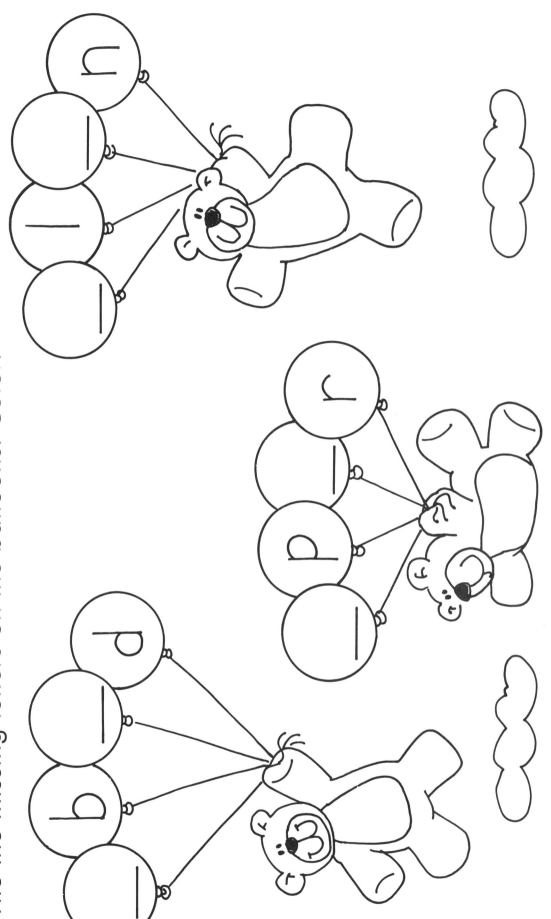

ABC Order © 1984 Monday Morning Books

Skill: ☐ b ☐ d

Cut and paste the missing letters in abc order. Color.

49

ABC Order © 1984 Monday Morning Books

Skill: □ b □

Write the lower case alphabet on the snake. Color.

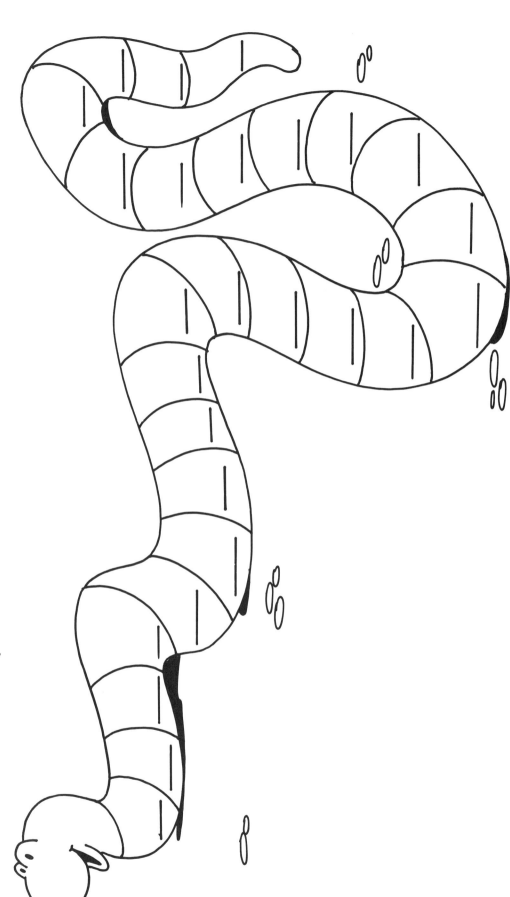

ABC Order © 1984 Monday Morning Books

Skill: a - z

Cut and paste to put the words in abc order.

kit

lot

elf

fin

ten

up

bat

cup

jet

ant

dot

sun

ABC Order © 1984 Monday Morning Books

Skill: words - first letter

Cut and paste to put the words in abc order. Color.

tap

net

rug

lip

dip

in

bag

gum

man

cab

sat

hen

52

Cut and paste to put the words in abc order. Color.

ABC Order © 1984 Monday Morning Books

Skill: words - first letter

Number the turtles to put the words in abc order.

ABC Order © 1984 Monday Morning Books

Name _____

Write the words on the trains in abc order. Color.

wig   ant   top

map   fun   bell

ABC Order © 1984 Monday Morning Books

Skill: words - first letter

Name _____

Write the words on the hats in abc order. Color.

1.
2.
3.

pat hum tap

1.
2.
3.

tan mill den

1.
2.
3.

lap band hop

56

ABC Order © 1984 Monday Morning Books

Skill: words - first letter

Name ___

Write the words on the magic hat in abc order. Color.

car

track

funny

lunch

1
2
3
4
5
6

book

jug

ABC Order © 1984 Monday Morning Books

Skill: words - first letter

57

Name _____

Cut and paste the missing word parts in abc order.

w___

w___

w___

w___

ell   in   ag   on

Skill: words - second letter

ABC Order © 1984 Monday Morning Books

58

Cut and paste the missing word parts in abc order.

s

s

s

s

s

od

et

at

un

ip

ABC Order © 1984 Monday Morning Books

Skill: words - second letter

Cut and paste the missing word parts in abc order.

oll

ip

pp

uck

ABC Order © 1984 Monday Morning Books

Skill: words - second letter

Name _____

Cut and paste the missing word parts in abc order.

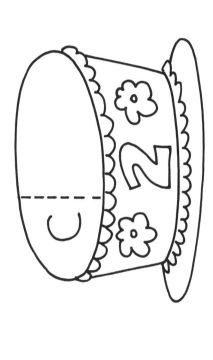

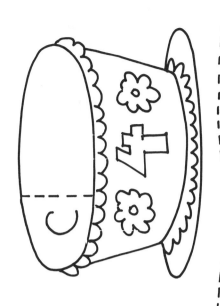

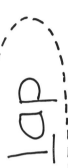

61

ABC Order © 1984 Monday Morning Books

Skill: words - second letter

Number the spaceships 1, 2, 3 to put them in abc order.

lamp

lock

let

___

___

jet

jam

job

___

___

___

plant

pet

pot

___

___

___

ram

rug

rest

___

___

___

3 grab

2 go

1 get

ABC Order © 1984 Monday Morning Books

Skill: words - second letter

Name <u>_</u>

Cut and paste the balls to put the words in abc order.

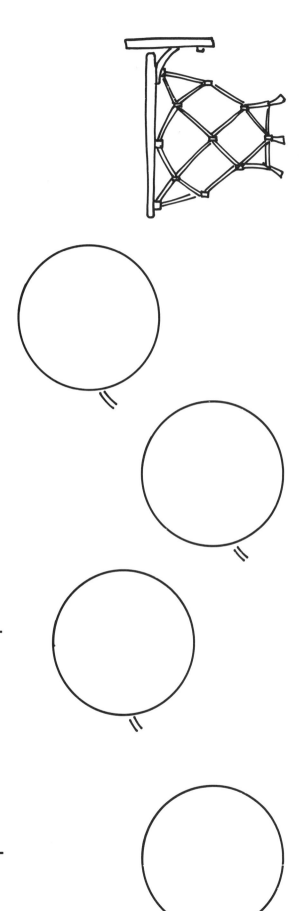

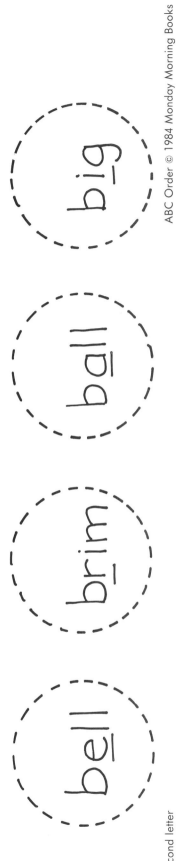

ABC Order © 1984 Monday Morning Books

Skill: words - second letter

Write the words on the ships in abc order. Color.

plan   pet   pin   pup

ABC Order © 1984 Monday Morning Books

Skill: words – second letter